"CRITTER FIELD"

written by

Marla J. Olszewski, PhD

Illustrated by

Kathy Kerber

AuthorHouse™
1663 Liberty Drive
Bloomington, IN 47403
www.authorhouse.com
Phone: 833-262-8899

This book is printed on acid-free paper.

ISBN: 978-1-4670-6721-8 (sc)

Library of Congress Control Number: 2011918815

Print information available on the last page.

Published by AuthorHouse 07/14/2022

authorHOUSE®

"CRITTER FIELD"

Written by Marla J. Olszewski, PhD, RMA

Illustrated by Kathy Kerber

Every day is a great day at Critter Field!

The buckeye tree is bustling with activity. Birds come to nest every spring. The "tweet, tweet, tweet" sounds like music in the morning. The apple tree and the pear tree have beautifully painted birdhouses hanging in them. They were painted by the little girl who lives in the blue cottage. The birds like to make their own nests in the buckeye tree.

The large pine trees lining the field are homes to the bunnies that live in Critter Field. Two of them are named "Thumper and Sheila". Sheila will stand on her hind legs and look like a kangaroo! Thumper is the chubby one. They will hop so close to the little girl and make her laugh. She is very happy to sit on the front porch and watch the critters scamper by.

The squirrel family runs all through the field and up and down the big oak tree to the willow tree on the other side. Big squirrels and little squirrels everywhere! They look like question marks with their loopy tails!

All year round, the family of crows comes to feast. The little girl's family feed them everyday. There is an area in Critter Field called "the crow plate" where all of the critter food goes. Not only crows eat from the crow plate, all of the animals in Critter Field do!

The lumbering raccoon family comes out at night. They are so chubby! They look like they are wearing little black masks when they look at you. They love to eat from the crow plate. Sometimes, the little girl will get so excited to see the lumbering raccoon, until he turns around and she sees that it is the wild cat, named No Tail. He runs from her!

Families of deer roam the field. Some just lay down in the soft grass and others graze through the field. Sometimes, there are four or five at a time. Big ones and small ones. Mommy deer and baby deer. They drink from the creek that runs through woods near Critter Field. They hide in the forest behind the little blue cottage.

During the hot summer months, a snake slithers through the field. He is afraid of the nearby family, though, so he stays hidden in the tall grass.

The little opossum wanders around at night also. He gets so close to the porch of the little blue cottage!

Chipmunks scamper free all through Critter Field!

Recently, a fat little groundhog wandered through the field! He must be new to the neighborhood! Sometimes the family in the little blue cottage watch the groundhog rolling in the grass during the day. Then he walks toward the forest eating clover.

Once, a fox went trotting up the road in front of the little blue cottage. Trot, trot, trot. He was orange and brown with a pointy nose. Don't get to close to Mr. Fox!

Sometimes guests come to visit Critter Field. They are named Molly and Luka. They are big, beautiful boxer dogs that are very playful! They live across the road from the little girl. Another guest who comes to visit named Mr. Pierce, is the local hawk that sits in the big oak tree waiting to swoop down and eat from the crow plate. Recently, Mr. Pierce has been bringing his own family to visit the field. There is a pretty Mrs. Pierce and a little baby! They spread their beautiful wings and soar through the air.

Mr. Skunk visits at night. One night when it was very dark, the family went outside to put food on the crow plate and Mr. Skunk was sitting right there next to the crow plate! The family stays away from Mr. Skunk!

Other night time visitors are the crickets! Music makers! The family will lie down in their beds at night and listen to the crickets until they fall asleep. The sound is so very peaceful! And the fireflies! They light up the yard! Little lightning bugs everywhere!

In the winter, the footprints are all through field! We wonder who is leaving all of these tracks? The family feeds the animals throughout the winter and the animals find the food buried in the snow. The family is happy to see that the critters eat throughout the winter!

The little girl that lives in the blue cottage loves the critters she sees everyday.

Winter, spring, summer or fall, it is always a great day at Critter Field!

The End

Printed in the United States
by Baker & Taylor Publisher Services